VERNIA JEAN

Jeremy Dugan McCloud

Small I May Be,
God Still Uses Me

This book belongs to
a totally cool person

- - - - - - - - - - - -
{your name}

To order additional copies of this book, contact:
Xlibris Corporation
1-888-795-4274
www.Xlibris.com
Orders@Xlibris.com

I was born for a purpose,
  a chosen design.
No one is like me!
  I am one of a kind.
Look at me now,
  what do you see?
Only an image
  of who I will be.
Who am I,
  this world changer to be?
My name is___*(your name)*___
Watch out world,
  you'll see more of me!

My name is Jeremy Dougan McCloud.
Oh, and the name! Well, my dad named me.
He says I'm pretty special
and I totally agree.

I am a little kid
as you can see.
But one thing you should know,
is that God uses me!

God uses us kids a lot!
He's doing it even now.
Just keep reading
and I'll show you how.

Small I may be,
God still uses me!

God uses me!

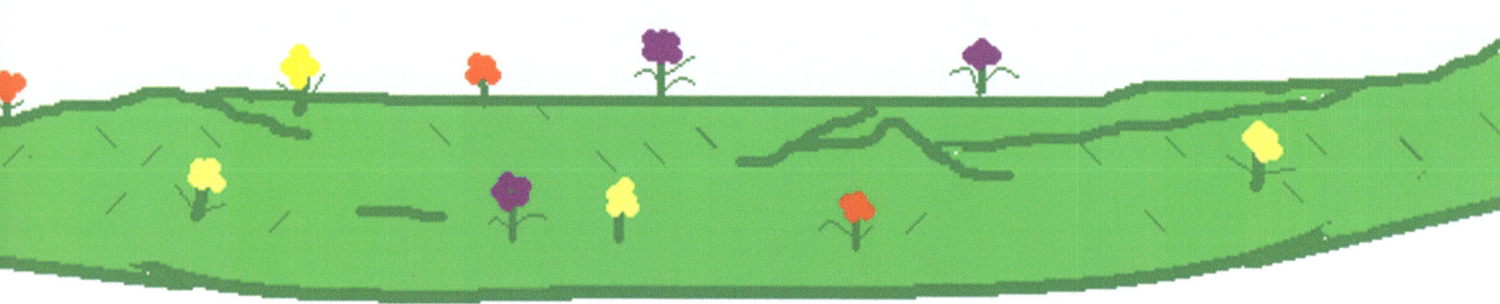

When I give mom a flower
from the neighbor's yard, or
for every one of my classmates
I make valentine cards

When I help my little sister tie
her shoes,

When I make friends with the
new kid at school.

God uses me!

When I give dad a big hug,
for helping me catch lightning bugs.

When I smile and say hello to the
people I meet.

When I kiss my sister or brother on
the cheek.

God uses me!

When I tell mom I'm sorry for breaking her favorite vase, and save my allowance to have it replaced.

When I wake early to make breakfast for mom and dad by myself,
And try to clean the mess without any help.

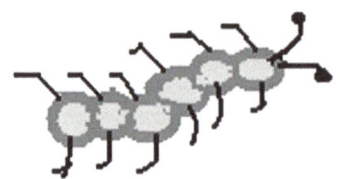

When I collect insects
Which is my favorite thing to do
Never again will I scare my sister
By putting them in her shoe

God uses me!

When I remind dad it's mom's birthday
And I help bake her cake

When dad takes me to the zoo, and I
invite my friends to go along too.

When mom asked who stuck their
finger in the chocolate cream pie
I admit, I did it
I choose not to lie.

God uses me!

When I clean my room without being told,

When I help mom with the laundry and the towels I fold.

When mom or dad come home from a long day of working hard, and I give them a big hug just because!

God uses me!

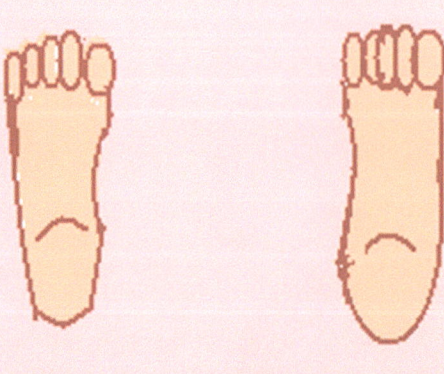

When I rub grandpa's aching feet
Or help grandma find her false teeth,

While sitting in the classroom, I
behave extremely nice,
and I choose not to punch the boy
who punched me
in my arm twice.

When I obey Mom and Dad

When I make someone happy
when they are sad

When I share with my friends

Whenever I give a helping hand

God uses me!

God uses me!

When I get on my knees
   and pray for mom, dad, classmates and friends.
The bully that pushed me down,
   while on the school grounds.
The girl that pulled my hair,
on a dare.
The girl that kicked me on the knee,
   my dog, my cat, or the bumblebee.

Even though I may seem,
   a handful at times to the extreme.
Small I may be,
   God still uses me!

The
End

Thanks for reading my story

Jeremy

Have you been helpful to your friends, family, or neighbors.